# Hippocrene

# CHILDREN'S
# ILLUSTRATED
# ITALIAN
# DICTIONARY

## ENGLISH · ITALIAN
## ITALIAN · ENGLISH

Compiled and translated by the Editors of Hippocrene Books

Interior illustrations by S. Grant (24, 81, 88); J. Gress (page 10, 21, 24, 37, 46, 54, 59, 65, 72, 75, 77);
K. Migliorelli (page 13, 14, 18, 19, 20, 21, 22, 25, 31, 32, 37, 39, 40, 46, 47, 66, 71, 75, 76, 82, 86, 87);
B. Swidzinska (page 9, 11, 12, 13, 14, 16, 23, 27, 28, 30, 32, 33, 35, 37, 38, 41, 42, 45, 46, 47, 48, 49, 50,
52, 53, 56, 57, 58, 59, 60, 61, 62, 63, 66, 68, 69, 70, 71, 72, 73, 75, 77, 78, 79, 83), N. Zhukov (page 8, 13,
14, 17, 18, 23, 27, 29, 33, 34, 39, 40, 41, 52, 64, 65, 71, 72, 73, 78, 84, 86, 88).

Design, prepress, and production: Graafiset International, Inc.

Cataloging-in-Publication Data available from the Library of Congress.

ISBN 0-7818-0771-9

Printed in Hong Kong.

For information, address:
Hippocrene Books, Inc.
171 Madison Avenue
New York, NY 10016

# INTRODUCTION

With their absorbent minds, infinite curiosities and excellent memories, children have enormous capacities to master many languages. All they need is exposure and encouragement.

The easiest way to learn a foreign language is to simulate the same natural method by which a child learns English. The natural technique is built on the concept that language is representational of concrete objects and ideas. The use of pictures and words are the natural way for children to begin to acquire a new language.

The concept of this Illustrated Dictionary is to allow children to build vocabulary and initial competency naturally. Looking at the pictorial content of the Dictionary and saying and matching the words in connection to the drawings gives children the opportunity to discover the foreign language and thus, a new way to communicate.

The drawings in the Dictionary are designed to capture children's imaginations and make the learning process interesting and entertaining, as children return to a word and picture repeatedly until they begin to recognize it.

*The beautiful images and clear presentation make this dictionary a wonderful tool for unlocking your child's multilingual potential.*

Deborah Dumont, M.A., M.Ed.,
Child Psychologist and Educational Consultant

# Italian Pronunciation

| Letter | Pronunciation system used |
|--------|---------------------------|
| a | **a** like the *a* in English 'far' |
| b | **b** like the *b* in English 'bar' |
| c (cc) | **k (kk)** like the *k* in English 'kite' or *c* in 'cat,' when followed by a, o, u |
| ch | **k** like *k* in English 'kite,' always followed by e, i |
| c | **tch** like *ch* in English 'china,' when followed by e, i |
| d | **d** like *d* in English 'door' |
| e | **è** like *e* in English 'ten' |
| e | **é** like *a* in English 'fate' |
| f | **f** like *f* in English 'fire' |
| g | **g** like *g* in English 'gang,' when followed by a, o, u |
| g | **j** like *j* in English 'jacket' or 'job' when followed by e or i |
| gh | **g** like *g* in English 'gang,' always followed by e or i |
| gli, gle | **ë** similar to *lli* in English 'billion' |
| gn | **ñ** similar to *ni* in English 'onion,' like the Spanish *ñ* in 'niño' |
| h | is always silent and mostly occurs in foreign words |
| i | **ee** like *i* in English 'machine' |
| l | **l** like *l* in English 'letter' |
| m | **m** like *m* in English 'mother' |
| n | **n** like *n* in English 'nut' |
| o | **o** like *o* in English 'spot' |
| p | **p** like *p* in English 'papaya' |
| qu | **koo** like *qu* in English 'quick' |
| r | **r** strongly rolled as in Spanish |
| s | **s** like *s* in English 'simple' |
| sc | **sh** like *sh* in English 'shame,' when followed by i or e |
| t | **t** like *t* in English 'torn' |
| u | **oo** like *oo* in English 'spoon' |
| | **v** like *v* in English 'victory' |
| z | **z** like *z* in English 'pizza' |
| z | **ds** like *ds* in English 'seeds' |

The stressed (accented) syllable is capitalized.

# *Articles*

| | |
|---|---|
| il | before masculine singular nouns |
| lo | before masculine singular nouns starting with s + consonant or z |
| l' | before masculine singular nouns starting with vowel |
| la | before feminine singular nouns |
| l' | before feminine singular nouns starting with a vowel |
| i | before masculine plural nouns |
| gli | before masculine plural nouns starting with s + consonant, z and vowel |
| le | before feminine plural nouns |

**airplane**      **(l') aeroplano**
*(l') a-e-ro-PLA-no*

**alligator**      **(il) alligatore**
*(eel) al-li-ga-TO-ré*

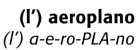

**alphabet**      **(l') alfabeto**
*(l') al-fa-BÈ-to*

**antelope**      **(l') antilope**
*(l') an-tee-LO-pé*

**antlers**      **(i) palchi**
*(ee) PAL-kee*

**apple**  **(la) mela**
*(la) MÉ-la*

**aquarium**  **(l') acquario**
*(l') a-KOO-a-ree-o*

**arch**  **(l') arco**
*(l') AR- ko*

**arrow**  **(la) freccia**
*(la) FRÉ-tcha*

**autumn**  **(l') autunno**
*(l') aoo-TOON-no*

**baby**  (il) **bebè**
*(eel) bé-BÉ*

**backpack**  (lo) **zaino**
*(lo) DSA-ee-no*

**badger**  (il) **tasso**
*(eel) TAHS-so*

**baker**  (il) **fornaio**
*(eel) for-NA-ee-o*

**ball**  (la) **palla**
*(la) PAL-la*

**balloon**  (il) **palloncino**
*(eel) pa-llon-TCHEE-no*

**banana**  **(la) banana**
*(la) ba-NA-na*

**barley**  **(l') orzo**
*(L') OR-dso*

**barrel**  **(la) botte**
*(la) BO-tté*

**basket**  **(il) cestino**
*(eel) tché-STEE-no*

**bat**  **(il) pipistrello**
*(eel) pee-pee-STRÈL-lo*

**beach**  **(la) spiaggia**
*(la) SPEE-A-ja*

**bear**　　　　　　**(l') orso**
*(L') OR-so*

**beaver**　　　　　　**(il) castoro**
*(eel) ka-STO-ro*

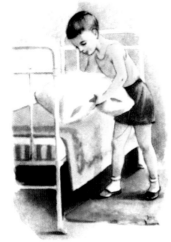

**bed**　　　　　　**(il) letto**
*(eel) LÈ-tto*

**bee**　　　　　　**(l') ape**
*(l') A-pé*

**beetle**　　　　　　**(lo) scarabeo**
*(lo) ska-ra-BÈ-o*

**bell**　　　　　　**(la) campanella**
*(la) kam-pa-NÈL-la*

**belt**  **(la) cintura**
*(la) tcheen-TOO-ra*

**bench**  **(la) panchina**
*(la) pan-KEE-na*

**bicycle**  **(la) bicicletta**
*(la) bee-tchee-KLÉ-tta*

**binoculars**  **(il) binocolo**
*(eel) bee-NO-ko-lo*

**bird**  **(l') uccello**
*(l') oo-TCHÈL-lo*

**birdcage**  **(la) gabbia**
*(la) GAB-bee-a*

**black** **nero**
*NÉ-ro*

**blocks** **(i) mattoni**
*(ee) ma-TTO-nee*

**blossom** **(il) fiore**
*(eel) FEE-o-ré*

**blue** **blu**
*bloo*

**boat** **(la) barca**
*(la) BAR-ka*

**bone** **(l') osso**
*(l') O-sso*

**book** **(il) libro**
*(eel) LEE-bro*

**boot** **(lo) stivale**
*(lo) stee-VA -lé*

**bottle** **(la) bottiglia**
*(la) bo-TEEL-yah*

**bowl** **(la) ciotola**
*(la) TCHEE-o-to-la*

**boy** **(il) ragazzo**
*(eel) ra-GA-zo*

**bracelet** **(il) braccialetto**
*(eel) bra-tcha-LÉ-tto*

**branch**      **(il) ramo**
*(eel) RA-mo*

**bread**      **(il) pane**
*(eel) PA-né*

**breakfast**      **(la) colazione**
*(la) ko-la-ZEE-o-né*

**bridge**      **(il) ponte**
*(eel) PON-té*

**broom**      **(la) scopa**
*(la) SKO-pa*

**brother**      **(il) fratello**
*(eel) fra-TÈL-lo*

**brown**     **marrone**
*mar-RO-né*

**brush**     **(la) spazzola**
*(la) SPAH-tsoh-la*

**bucket**     **(il) secchio**
*(eel) SÉ-kee-o*

**bulletin board**     **la) bacheca**
*(la) ba-KÈ-ka*

**bumblebee**     **(il) calabrone**
*(eel) ka-la-BRO-né*

**butterfly**     **(la) farfalla**
*(la) far-FAL-la*

**cab**            **(il) taxi**
*(eel) TA-ksee*

**cabbage**        **(il) cavolo**
*(eel) KA-vo-lo*

**cactus**           **(il) cactus**
*(eel) KAK-toos*

**café**             **(il) bar**
*(eel) bar*

**cake**            **(la) torta**
*(la) TOR-ta*

**camel**         **(il) cammello**
*(eel) kam-MÈL-lo*

**camera  (la) macchinetta fotografica**
*(la) ma-kkee-NÉ-tta fo-to-GRA-fee-ka*

**candle  (la) candela**
*(la) kan-DÉ-la*

**candy  (il) dolciume**
*(eel) dohl-TCHOO-me*

**canoe  (la) canoa**
*(la) ka-NO-a*

**cap  (il) berretto**
*(eel) bé-RRÉ-tto*

**captain  (il) capitano**
*(eel) ka-pee-TA-no*

**car**     **(la) macchina**
*(la) MA-kkee-na*

**card**     **(la) carta**
*(la) KAR-ta*

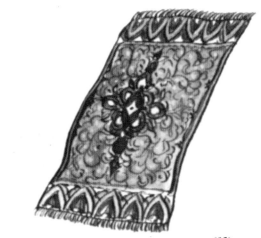

**carpet**     **(il) tappeto**
*(eel) tap-PÉ-to*

**carrot**     **(la) carota**
*(la) ka-RO-ta*

**(to) carry**     **portare**
*por-TA-ré*

**castle**     **(il) castello**
*(eel) ka-STÈ-lo*

**cat** **(il) gatto**
*(eel) GA-tto*

**cave** **(la) grotta**
*(la) GRO-tta*

**chair** **(la) sedia**
*(la) SÈ-dee-a*

**cheese** **(il) formaggio**
*(eel) for-MA-jo*

**cherry** **(la) ciliegia**
*(la) tchee-LEE-È-ja*

**chimney** **(il) fumaiolo**
*(eel) foo-mah-YOH-lo*

**chocolate**     **(la) cioccolata**
*(la) tcho-kko-LA-ta*

**Christmas tree**   **(l') albero di Natale**
*(L') AL-bé-ro dee na-TA-lé*

**circus**     **(il) circo**
*(eel) TCHEER-ko*

**(to) climb**     **arrampicarsi**
*ar-ram-pee-KAR-see*

**cloud**     **(la) nuvola**
*(la) NOO-vo-la*

**clown**     **(il) pagliaccio**
*(eel) pa-ËA-tcho*

**coach**     **(la) carrozza**
*(la) kar-RO-za*

**coat**     **(il) cappotto**
*(eel) kap-PO-tto*

**coconut**     **(il) cocco**
*(eel) KO-kko*

**comb**     **(il) pettine**
*(eel) PÈ-ttee-né*

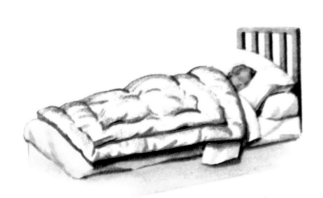

**comforter**     **(il) piumino**
*(eel) pee-oo-ME-no*

**compass**     **(la) bussola**
*(la) BOO-sso-la*

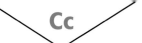

**(to) cook**        **cucinare**
*koo-tchee-NA-ré*

**cork**        **(il) tappo**
*(eel) TAP-po*

**corn**        **(la) pannocchia**
*(la) pan-NO-kkee-a*

**cow**        **(la) mucca**
*(la) MOO-kka*

**cracker**        **(il) biscotto**
*(eel) bees-KOH-to*

**cradle**        **(la) culla**
*(la) KOOL-la*

**(to) crawl**     **andar carponi**
*an-DAR kar-PO-nee*

**(to) cross**     **attraversare**
*a-ttra-vér-SA-ré*

**crown**     **(la) corona**
*(la) ko-RO-na*

**(to) cry**     **piangere**
*PEE-AN-jé-ré*

**cucumber**     **(il) cetriolo**
*(eel) tché-TREE-o-lo*

**curtain**     **(la) cortina**
*(la) kor-TEE-na*

**(to) dance**  **ballare**
*bal-LA-ré*

**dandelion**  **(il) dente di leone**
*(eel) DÈN-té dee lé-O-né*

**date**  **(la) data**
*(la) DA-ta*

**deer**  **(il) cerbiatto**
*(eel) tchér-BEE-A-tto*

**desert**  **(il) deserto**
*(eel) dé-SÈR-to*

**desk**  **(il) banco**
*(eel) BAN-ko*

**dirty**  **sporco**
*SPOR-ko*

**dog**

**(il) cane**
*(eel) KA-né*

**doghouse**    **(la) cuccia**
*(la) KOO-tcha*

**doll**

**(la) bambola**
*(la) BAM-bo-la*

**dollhouse**    **(la) casa della bambola**
*(la) KA-sa dél-la BAM-bo-la*

**dolphin**

**(il) delfino**
*(eel) dél-FEE-no*

**donkey**

**(l') asino**
*(L') A-see-no*

**dragon**

**(il) drago**
*(eel) DRA-go*

**dragonfly**　　　　　**(la) libellula**
*(la) lee-BÈL-loo-la*

**(to) draw**　　　　　**disegnare**
*dee-sé-ÑA-ré*

**dress**　　　　　**(il) vestito**
*(eel) vé-STEE-to*

**(to) drink**　　　　　**bere**
*BÉ-ré*

**drum**　　　　　**(il) tamburo**
*(eel) tam-BOO-ro*

**duck**　　　　　**(l') anatra**
*(L') A-na-tra*

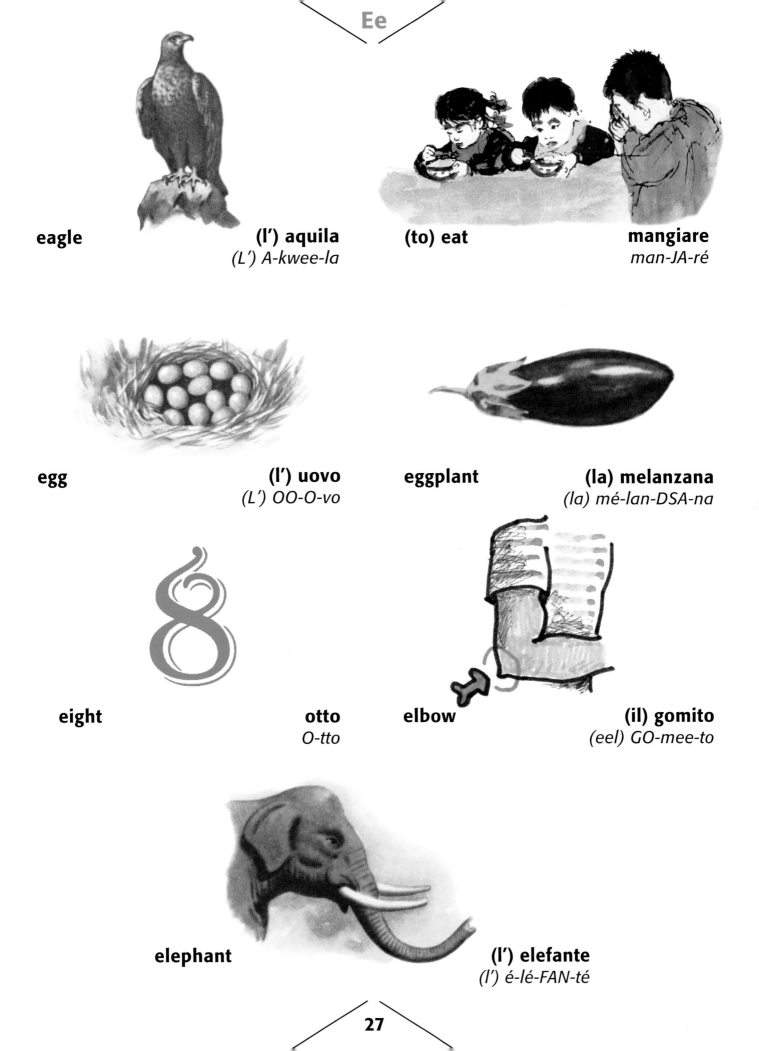

**eagle**     **(l') aquila**
*(L') A-kwee-la*

**(to) eat**     **mangiare**
*man-JA-ré*

**egg**     **(l') uovo**
*(L') OO-O-vo*

**eggplant**     **(la) melanzana**
*(la) mé-lan-DSA-na*

**eight**     **otto**
*O-tto*

**elbow**     **(il) gomito**
*(eel) GO-mee-to*

**elephant**     **(l') elefante**
*(l') é-lé-FAN-té*

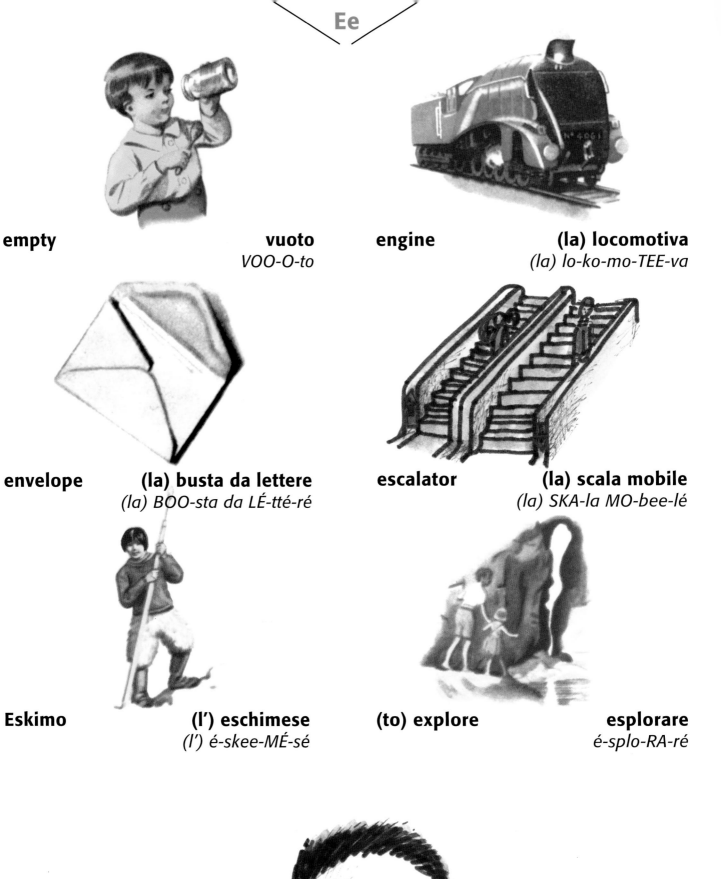

**empty**     **vuoto**
*VOO-O-to*

**engine**     **(la) locomotiva**
*(la) lo-ko-mo-TEE-va*

**envelope**     **(la) busta da lettere**
*(la) BOO-sta da LÉ-tté-ré*

**escalator**     **(la) scala mobile**
*(la) SKA-la MO-bee-lé*

**Eskimo**     **(l') eschimese**
*(l') é-skee-MÉ-sé*

**(to) explore**     **esplorare**
*é-splo-RA-ré*

**eye**     **(l') occhio**
*(L') OK-kee-o*

**face**      **(il) viso**
*(eel) VEE-so*

**fan**      **(il) ventilatore**
*(eel) vén-tee-la-TO-ré*

**father**      **(il) papà**
*(eel) pa-PÀ*

**fear**      **(la) paura**
*(la) pa-OO-ra*

**feather**      **(la) piuma**
*(la) PEE-OO-ma*

**(to) feed**      **dar da mangiare**
*dar da man-JA-ré*

**fence** **(la) staccionata**
*(la) sta-tcho-NA-ta*

**fern** **(la) felce**
*(la) FÉL-tché*

**field** **(il) campo**
*(eel) KAM-po*

**field mouse** **(il) topolino**
*(eel) to-po-LEE-no*

**finger** **(il) dito**
*(eel) DEE-to*

**fir tree** **(l') abete**
*(l') a-BÉ-té*

**fire**     **(il) fuoco**
*(eel) FOO-O-ko*

**fish**     **(il) pesce**
*(eel) PÉ-shé*

**(to) fish**     **pescare**
*pé-SKA-ré*

**fist**     **(il) pugno**
*(eel) POO-ño*

**five**     **cinque**
*TCHEEN-koo-é*

**flag**     **(la) bandiera**
*(la) ban-DEE-È-ra*

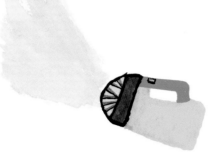

**flashlight**     **(la) torcia elettrica**
*(la) TOR-tcha é-LÈ-ttree-ka*

**(to) float**     **galleggiare**
*gal-lé-JA-ré*

**flower**     **(il) fiore**
*(eel) FEE-O-ré*

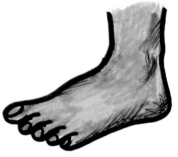

**(to) fly**     **volare**
*vo-LA-ré*

**foot**     **(il) piede**
*(eel) PEE-È-dé*

**fork**     **(la) forchetta**
*(la) for-KÉ-tta*

**fountain**     **(la) fontana**
*(la) fon-TA-na*

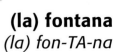

**four**      **quattro**
*KOO-A-ttro*

**fox**      **(la) volpe**
*(la) VOL-pé*

**frame**      **(la) cornice**
*(la) kor-NEE-tché*

**friend**      **(l') amico**
*(l') a-MEE-ko*

**frog**      **(la) rana**
*(la) RA-na*

**fruit**      **(la) frutta**
*(la) FROO-tta*

**furniture**      **(i) mobili**
*(ee) MO-bee-lee*

**garden**     **(il) giardino**
*(eel) jar-DEE-no*

**gate**     **(il) cancello**
*(eel) kan-TCHÈL-lo*

**(to) gather**     **raccogliere**
*ra-KKO-ëëré*

**geranium**     **(il) geranio**
*(eel) jé-RA-nee-o*

**giraffe**     **(la) giraffa**
*(la) jee-RAF-fa*

**girl**     **(la) ragazza**
*(la) ra-GA-za*

**(to) give**　　　　　**dare**
*DA-ré*

**glass**　　　　　**(il) bicchiere**
*(eel) bee-KKEE-È-ré*

**glasses**　　　　　**(gli) occhiali**
*(ëee) o-KKEE-A-lee*

**globe**　　　　　**(il) globo**
*(eel) GLO-bo*

**glove**　　　　　**(il) guanto**
*(eel) GOO-AN-to*

**goat**　　　　　**(la) capra**
*(la) KA-pra*

**goldfish**      **(il) pesciolino rosso**
*(eel) pé-sho-LEE-no ro-sso*

**"Good Night"**      **"Buona notte"**
*"BOO-O-na NO-tté"*

**"Good-bye"**      **"Addio"**
*"A-DEE-o"*

**goose**      **(l') oca**
*(l') O-ka*

**grandfather**      **(il) nonno**
*(eel) NON-no*

**grandmother**      **(la) nonna**
*(la) NON-na*

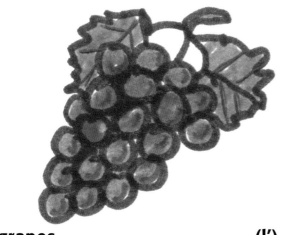

**grapes** **(l') uva**
*(l') OO-va*

**grasshopper** **(il) grillo**
*(eel) GREEL-lo*

**green** **verde**
*VÈR-dé*

**greenhouse** **(la) serra**
*(la) SÈR-ra*

**guitar** **(la) chitarra**
*(la) kee-TAR-ra*

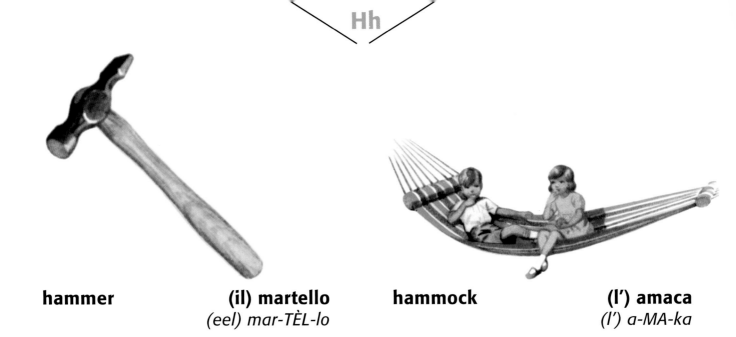

**hammer**　　　**(il) martello**
*(eel) mar-TÈL-lo*

**hammock**　　　**(l') amaca**
*(l') a-MA-ka*

**hamster**　　　**(il) criceto**
*(eel) kree-TCHÉ-to*

**hand**　　　**(la) mano**
*(la) MA-no*

**handbag**　　　**(la) borsetta**
*(la) bor-SÉ-tta*

**handkerchief**　　　**(il) fazzoletto**
*(eel) fa-zo-LÉ-tto*

**harvest**     **(il) raccolto**
*(eel) ra-KKOL-to*

**hat**     **(il) cappello**
*(eel) kap-PÈL-lo*

**hay**     **(il) fieno**
*(eel) FEE-EH-no*

**headdress**     **(il) copricapo**
*(eel) ko-pree-KA-po*

**heart**     **(il) cuore**
*(eel) KOO-O-ré*

**hedgehog**     **(il) porcospino**
*(eel) POR-ko-SPEE-no*

**hen**      **(la) gallina**
*(la) gal-LEE-na*

**(to) hide**      **nascondersi**
*na-SKON-dér-see*

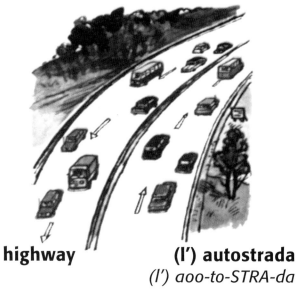
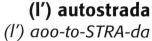

**highway**      **(l') autostrada**
*(l') aoo-to-STRA-da*

**honey**      **(il) miele**
*(eel) MEE-È-lé*

**horns**      **(le) corna**
*(lé) KOR-na*

**horse**      **(il) cavallo**
*(eel) ka-VAL-lo*

**horseshoe** **(il) ferro di cavallo**
*(eel) FÈR-ro dee ka-VAL-lo*

**hourglass** **(la) clessidra**
*(la) kle-SSEE-dra*

**house** **(la) casa**
*(la) KA-sa*

**(to) hug** **abbracciare**
*ab-bra-TCHA-ré*

**hydrant** **(l') idrante**
*(l') ee-DRAN-té*

**ice cream**　　　**(il) gelato**
*(eel) jé-LA-to*

**ice cubes**　　**(i) cubetti di ghiaccio**
*(ee) koo-BÉ-ttee dee GEE-A-tcho*

**ice-skating**　　　**pattinare sul ghiaccio**
*pa-ttee-NA-ré sool GEE-A-tcho*

**instrument**　　**(lo) strumento**
*(lo) stroo-MÉN-to*

**iris**　　　　　　**(l') iris**
*(L') EE-rees*

**iron**　　**(il) ferro da stiro**
*(eel) FÈR-ro da STEE-ro*

**island**　　　　**(l') isola**
*(L') EE-so-la*

**jacket**      **(la) giacca**
*(la) JA-kka*

**jam**      **(la) marmellata**
*(la) mar-mél-LA-ta*

**jigsaw puzzle**      **(il) puzzle**
*(eel) PA-sl*

**jockey**      **(il) fantino**
*(eel) fan-TEE-no*

**juggler**      **(il) giocoliere**
*(eel) jo-ko-LEE-È-ré*

**(to) jump**      **saltare**
*sal-TA-ré*

**kangaroo**     **(il) canguro**
*(eel) kan-GOO-ro*

**key**     **(la) chiave**
*(la) KEE-A-vé*

**kitten**     **(il) gattino**
*(eel) ga-TTEE-no*

**knife**     **(il) coltello**
*(eel) kol-TÈL-lo*

**knight**     **(il) cavaliere**
*(eel) ka-va-LEE-È-ré*

**(to) knit**     **lavorare a maglia**
*la-vo-RA-ré a MA-ëa*

**knot**     **(il) nodo**
*(eel) NO-do*

**koala bear**     **(il) koala**
*(eel) KO-A-la*

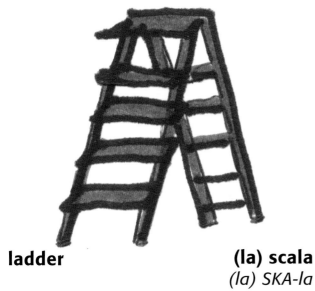

**ladder**     **(la) scala**
*(la) SKA-la*

**ladybug**     **(la) coccinella**
*(la) ko-tchee-NÈL-la*

**lamb**     **(l') agnellino**
*(l') a-ñél-LEE-no*

**lamp**     **(la) lampada**
*(la) LAM-pa-da*

**(to) lap**     **leccare**
*lé-KKA-ré*

**laughter**     **(la) risata**
*(la) ree-SA-ta*

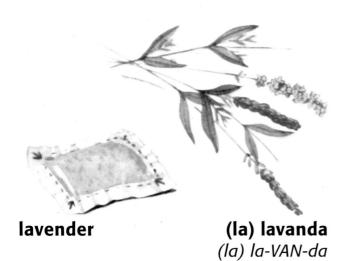

**lavender**      **(la) lavanda**
*(la) la-VAN-da*

**lawn mower**      **(il) tosaerba**
*(eel) to-sa-ÈR-ba*

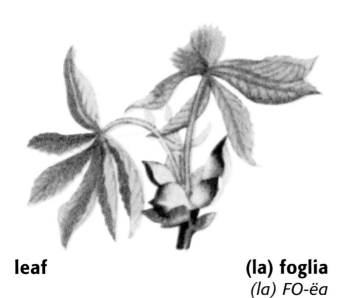

**leaf**      **(la) foglia**
*(la) FO-ëa*

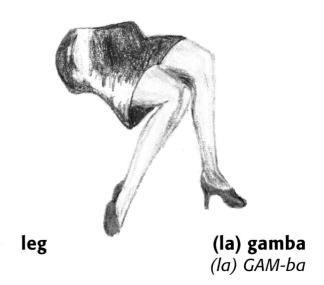

**leg**      **(la) gamba**
*(la) GAM-ba*

**lemon**      **(il) limone**
*(eel) lee-MO-né*

**lettuce**      **(la) lattuga**
*(la) la-TTOO-ga*

**lightbulb**  **(la) lampadina**
*(la) lam-pa-DEE-na*

**lighthouse**  **(il) faro**
*(eel) FA-ro*

**lilac**  **(il) lillà**
*(eel) lee-LLÀ*

**lion**  **(il) leone**
*(eel) lé-O-né*

**(to) listen**  **ascoltare**
*a-skol-TA-ré*

**lobster**  **(l') aragosta**
*(l') a-ra-GO-sta*

**lock**      **(la) serratura**
*(la) sér-ra-TOO-ra*

**lovebird**      **(l') inseparabile**
*(l') een-sé-pa-RA-bee-lé*

**luggage**      **(le) valige**
*(lé) va-LEE-jé*

**lumberjack**      **(il) tagliaboschi**
*(eel) ta-ëa-BO-skee*

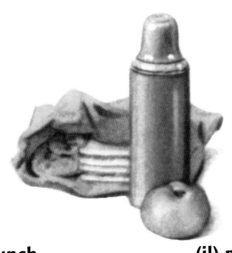

**lunch**      **(il) pranzo**
*(eel) PRAN-zo*

**lynx**      **(la) lince**
*(la) LEEN-tché*

**magazine**  **il) giornaletto**
*(eel) jor-na-LÉ-tto*

**magician**  **(il) prestigiatore**
*(eel) pré-stee-ja-TO-ré*

**magnet**  **(la) calamita**
*(la) ka-la-MEE-ta*

**map**  **(la) cartina geografica**
*(la) kar-TEE-na jéo-GRA-fee-ka*

**maple leaf**  **(la) foglia d'acero**
*(la) FO-ëa D-A-tché-ro*

**marketplace**  **(il) mercato**
*(eel) mér-KA-to*

**mask**  **(la) maschera**
*(la) MA-ské-ra*

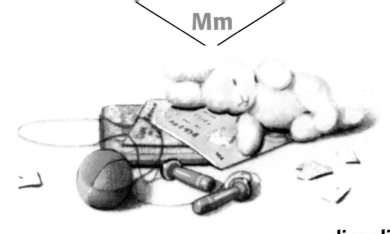

**messy**

**disordinato**
*dee-sor-dee-NA-to*

**milkman**

**(il) lattaio**
*(eel) la-TTA-ee-o*

**mirror**

**(lo) specchio**
*(lo) SPÈ-kkee-o*

**mitten**

**(il) mezzo guanto**
*(eel) ME-dso GWAHN-to*

**money**

**(i) soldi**
*(ee) SOL-dee*

**monkey**

**(la) scimmia**
*(la) SHEE-mmee-a*

**moon**

**(la) luna**
*(la) LOO-na*

**mother**　　　　**(la) mamma**
*(la) MAM-ma*

**mountain**　　　　**(la) montagna**
*(la) mon-TA-ña*

**mouse**　　　　**(il) topo**
*(eel) TO-po*

**mouth**　　　　**(la) bocca**
*(la) BO-kka*

**mushroom**　　　　**(il) fungo**
*(eel) FOON-go*

**music**　　　　**(la) musica**
*(la) MOO-see-ka*

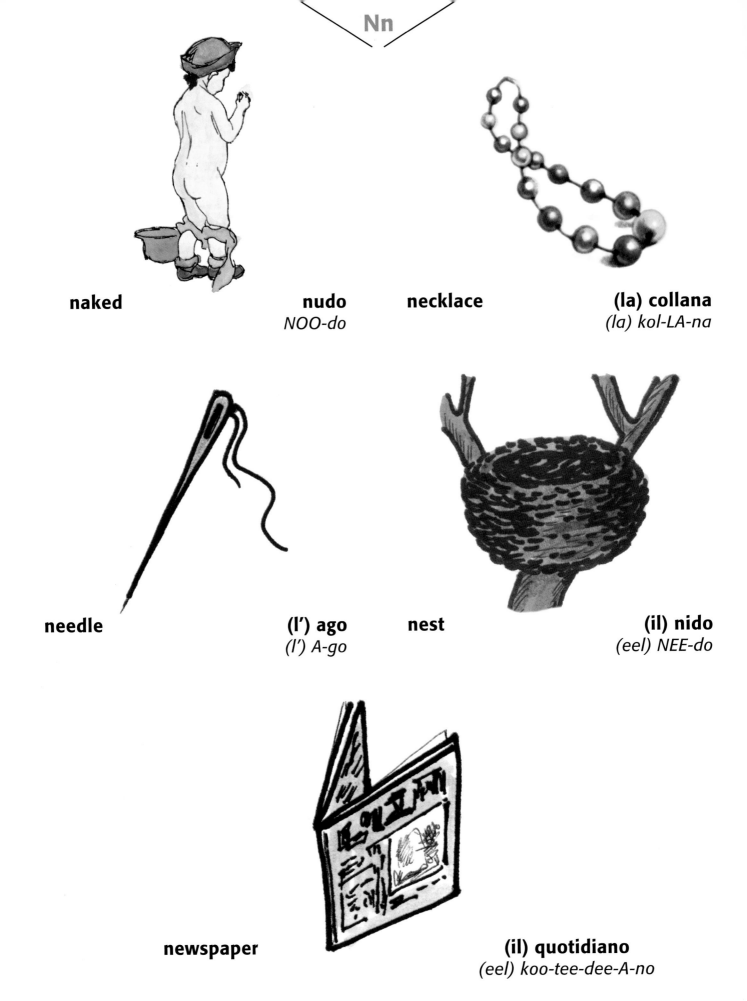

**naked**     **nudo**
*NOO-do*

**necklace**     **(la) collana**
*(la) kol-LA-na*

**needle**     **(l') ago**
*(l') A-go*

**nest**     **(il) nido**
*(eel) NEE-do*

**newspaper**     **(il) quotidiano**
*(eel) koo-tee-dee-A-no*

**nightingale**      **(l') usignolo**
*(l') oo-see-ÑO-lo*

**nine**      **nove**
*NO-vé*

**notebook**      **(il) quaderno**
*(eel) koo-a-DÈR-no*

**number**      **(il) numero**
*(eel) NOO-mé-ro*

**nut**      **(la) noce**
*(la) NO-tché*

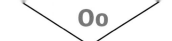
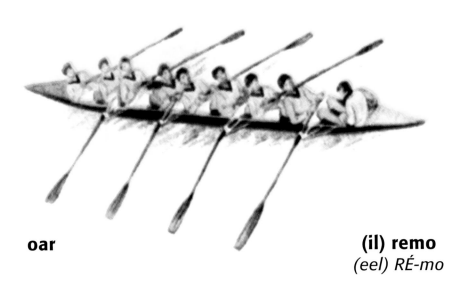

**oar**        **(il) remo**
*(eel) RÉ-mo*

**ocean liner**    **(la) nave da crociera**
*(la) NA-vé da kro-TCHÈ-ra*

**old**        **vecchio**
*VE-kkee-o*

**1**

**one**      **uno**
*OO-no*

**onion**      **(la) cipolla**
*(la) tchee-POL-la*

**open**        **aperto**
*a-PÈR-to*

**orange**        **(l') arancia**
*(l') a-RAN-tcha*

**ostrich**        **(lo) struzzo**
*(lo) STROO-zo*

**owl**        **(la) civetta**
*(la) tchee-VÉ-tta*

**ox**        **(il) bue**
*(eel) BOO-é*

**padlock**      **(il) lucchetto**
*(eel) loo-KKÉ-tto*

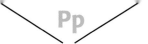

**paint**      **(i) colori**
*(ee) ko-LO-ree*

**painter**      **(il) pittore**
*(eel) pee-TTO-ré*

**pajamas**      **(il) pyjama**
*(eel) pee-ja-ma*

**palm tree**      **(la) palma**
*(la) PAL-ma*

**paper**      **(la) carta**
*(la) KAR-ta*

**parachute**      **(il) paracadute**
*(eel) pa-ra-ka-DOO-té*

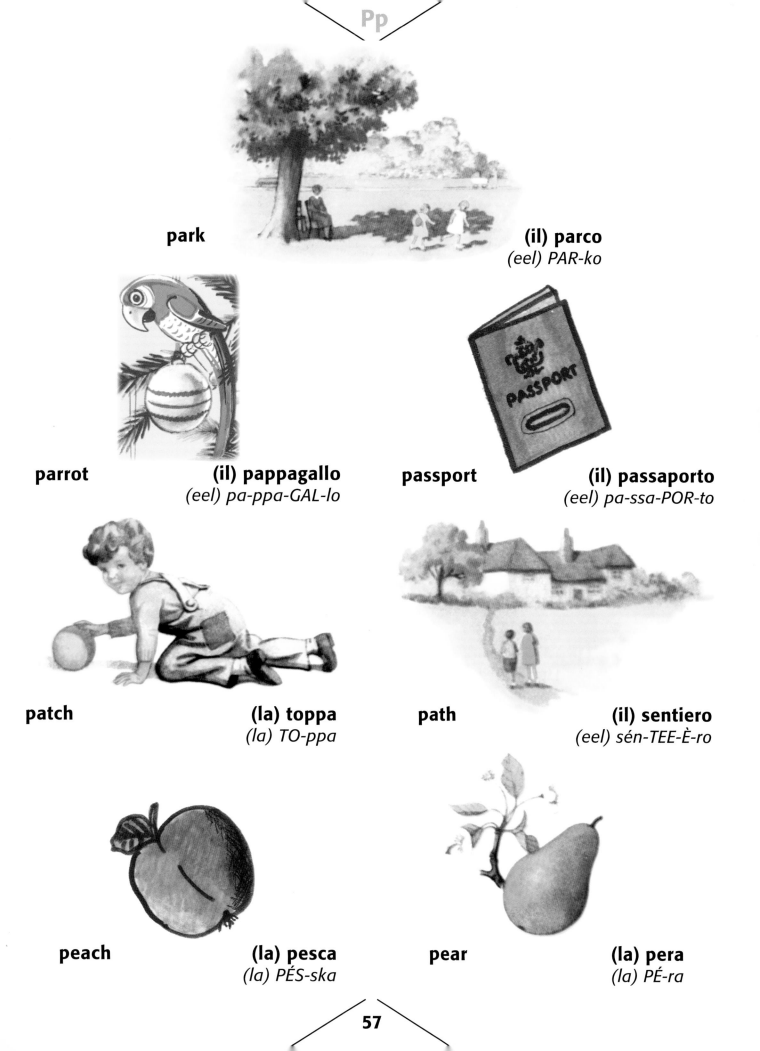

park     **(il) parco**
*(eel) PAR-ko*

parrot     **(il) pappagallo**
*(eel) pa-ppa-GAL-lo*

passport     **(il) passaporto**
*(eel) pa-ssa-POR-to*

patch     **(la) toppa**
*(la) TO-ppa*

path     **(il) sentiero**
*(eel) sén-TEE-È-ro*

peach     **(la) pesca**
*(la) PÉS-ska*

pear     **(la) pera**
*(la) PÉ-ra*

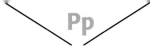

**pebble**

**(il) ciottolo**
*(eel) TCHO-tto-lo*

**(to) peck**

**beccare**
*bé-KKA-ré*

**(to) peel**

**sbucciare**
*sboo-TCHA-ré*

**pelican**

**(il) pellicano**
*(eel) pél-lee-KA-no*

**pencil**

**(la) matita**
*(la) ma-TEE-ta*

**penguin**

**(il) pinguino**
*(eel) peen-GOO-EE-no*

**people**

**(la) gente**
*(la) JÈN-té*

**piano** | **(il) pianoforte**
*(eel) pee-a-no-FOR-té*

**pickle** | **(il) cetriolo sottaceto**
*(eel) tché-TREE0-LO so-tta-TCHÉ-to*

**pie** | **(la) crostata**
*(la) kro-STA-ta*

**pig** | **(il) maiale**
*(eel) ma-EE-A-lé*

**pigeon** | **(il) piccione**
*(eel) pee-TCHO-né*

**pillow** | **(il) cuscino**
*(eel) koo-SHEE-no*

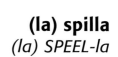

**pin** | **(la) spilla**
*(la) SPEEL-la*

**pine**      **(il) pino**
*(eel) PEE-no*

**pineapple**      **(l') ananasso**
*(l') a-na-NAS-so*

**pit**      **(il) nocciolo**
*(eel) NÓ-tcho-lo*

**pitcher**      **(la) brocca**
*(la) BRO-kka*

**plate**      **(il) piatto**
*(eel) PEE-A-tto*

**platypus**      **(l') ornitorinco**
*(l') or-nee-to-REEN-ko*

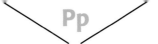

**(to) play**  **giocare**
*jo-KA-ré*

**plum**  **(la) prugna**
*(la) PROO-ña*

**polar bear**  **(l') orso polare**
*(l') or-so po-LA-ré*

**pony**  **(il) pony**
*(eel) PO-nee*

**pot**  **(la) padella**
*(la) pa-DÈL-la*

**potato**  **(la) patata**
*(la) pa-TA-ta*

**(to) pour**     **versare**
*vér-SA-ré*

**present**     **(il) regalo**
*(eel) ré-GA-lo*

**(to) pull**     **tirare**
*tee-RA-ré*

**pumpkin**     **(la) zucca**
*(la) DSOO-kka*

**Qq**

**puppy**     **(il) cucciolo**
*(eel) KOO-tcho-lo*

**queen**     **(la) regina**
*(la) ré-JEE-na*

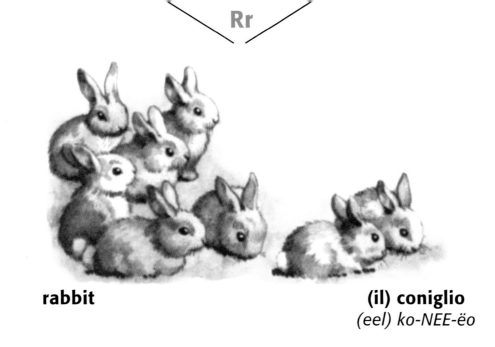

**rabbit**

**(il) coniglio**
*(eel) ko-NEE-ëo*

**raccoon**

**(il) procione**
*(eel) pro-TCHO-né*

**racket**

**(la) racchetta**
*(la) ra-KKÉ-tta*

**radio**

**(la) radio**
*(la) RA-dee-o*

**radish**

**(il) ravanello**
*(eel) ra-va-NÈ-llo*

**raft** **(la) zattera**
*(la) ZAT-te-ra*

**rain** **(la) pioggia**
*(la) PEE-O-ja*

**rainbow** **(l') arcobaleno**
*(l') ar-ko-ba-LÉ-no*

**raincoat** **(l') impermeabile**
*(l') eem-pér-mé-A-bee-lé*

**raspberry** **(il) lampone**
*(eel) lam-PO-né*

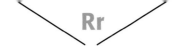

**(to) read**      **leggere**
*LÈ-jé-ré*

**red**      **rosso**
*RO-sso*

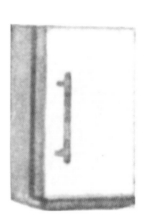

**refrigerator**      **(il) frigorifero**
*(eel) free-go-REE-fé-ro*

**rhinoceros**      **(il) rinoceronte**
*(eel) ree-no-tché-RON-té*

**ring**      **(l') anello**
*(l') a-NÈL-lo*

**(to) ring**   suonare
*soo-o-NA-ré*

river   **(il) fiume**
*(eel) FEE-OO-mé*

**road**   **(la) strada**
*(la) STRA-da*

rocket   **(il) razzo**
*(eel) RA-dso*

**roof**   **(il) tetto**
*(eel) TÉ-tto*

rooster   **(il) gallo**
*(eel) GALL-o*

**root**      **(la) radice**
*(la) RA-dee-tché*

**rope**      **(la) corda**
*(la) KOR-da*

**rose**      **(la) rosa**
*(la) RO-sa*

**(to) row**      **remare**
*ré-MA-ré*

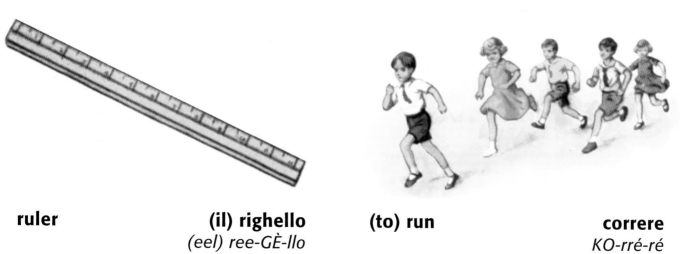

**ruler**      **(il) righello**
*(eel) ree-GÈ-llo*

**(to) run**      **correre**
*KO-rré-ré*

**safety pin**　　**(la) spilla da balia**
*(la) SPEE-lla da BÀ-lee-a*

**(to) sail**　　**navigare**
*na-vi-GA-ré*

**sailor**　　**(il) marinaio**
*(eel) ma-ree-NA-ee-o*

**salt**　　**(il) sale**
*(eel) SA-lé*

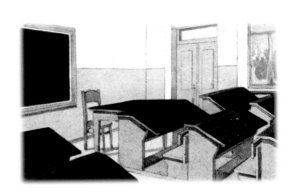

**scarf**　　**(la) sciarpa**
*(la) SHAR-pa*

**school**　　**(la) scuola**
*(la) SKOO-O-la*

**scissors** **(le) forbici**
*(lé) FOR-bee-tchee*

**screwdriver** **(il) cacciavite**
*(eel) ka-tcha-VEE-té*

**seagull** **(il) gabbiano**
*(eel) ga-BBEE-a-no*

**seesaw** **(l') altalena**
*(l') al-ta-LÉ-na*

**seven** **sette**
*SÈ-tté*

**(to) sew** **cucire**
*koo-TCHEE-ré*

**shark**      **(lo) squalo**
*(lo) SKOO-A-lo*

**sheep**      **(la) pecora**
*(la) PÈ-ko-ra*

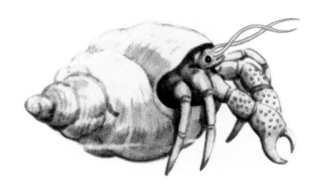

**shell**      **(la) conchiglia**
*(la) kon-KEE-ëa*

**shepherd**      **(il) pastore**
*(eel) pa-STO-ré*

**ship**      **(la) nave**
*(la) NA-vé*

**shirt**      **(la) camicia**
*(la) ka-MEE-tcha*

**shoe**  **(la) scarpa**
*(la) SKAR-pa*

**shovel**  **(la) pala**
*(la) PA-la*

**(to) show**  **mostrare**
*mo-STRA-ré*

**shower**  **(la) doccia**
*(la) DO-tcha*

**shutter**  **(l') imposta**
*(l') eem-PO-sta*

**sick**  **malato**
*ma-LA-to*

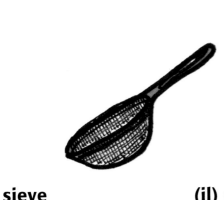

**sieve**      **(il) passino**
*(eel) pa-SSEE-no*

**(to) sing**      **cantare**
*kan-TA-ré*

**(to) sit**      **sedere**
*sé-DÉ-ré*

**six**      **sei**
*SÈ-ee*

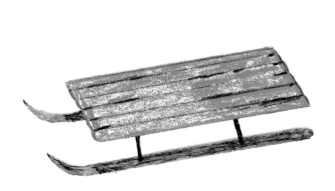

**sled**      **(la) slitta**
*(la) ZLEET-ta*

**(to) sleep**      **dormire**
*dor-MEE-ré*

**small** **piccolo**
*PEE-kko-lo*

**smile** **(il) sorriso**
*(eel) so-RREE-so*

**snail** **(la) lumaca**
*(la) loo-MA-ka*

**snake** **(il) serpente**
*(eel) sér-PÈN-té*

**snow** **(la) neve**
*(la) NÉ-vé*

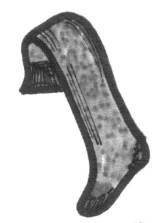

**sock** **(il) pedalino**
*(eel) pé-da-LEE-no*

**sofa**      **(il) divano**
*(eel) dee-VA-no*

**sparrow**      **(il) passero**
*(eel) PA-ssé-ro*

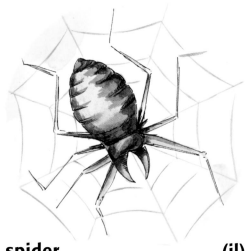

**spider**      **(il) ragno**
*(eel) RA-ño*

**spiderweb**      **(la) ragnatela**
*(la) ra-ña-TÉ-la*

**spoon**      **(il) cucchiaio**
*(eel) koo-KKEE-A-ee-o*

**squirrel**      **(lo) scoiattolo**
*(lo) sko-ee-a-TTO-lo*

**stairs**　　**(le) scale**
*(lé) SKA-lé*

**stamp**　　**(il) francobollo**
*(eel) fran-ko-BO-llo*

**starfish**　　**(la) stella marina**
*(la) STÉL-la ma-REE-na*

**stork**　　**(la) cicogna**
*(la) tchee-KO-ña*

**stove**　　**(la) macchina del gas**
*(la) MA-kkee-na dél GAS*

**strawberry**　　**(la) fragola**
*(la) FRA-go-la*

**subway** **(la) metropolitana**
*(la) mè-tro-po-lee-TA-na*

**sugar cube   (la) zolletta di zucchero**
*(la) dso-LLÉ-tta dee DSOO-kké-ro*

**sun** **(il) sole**
*(eel) SO-lé*

**sunflower** **(il) girasole**
*(eel) jee-ra-SO-lé*

**sweater** **(il) maglione**
*(eel) ma-ËO-né*

**(to) sweep** **spazzare**
*spa-ZA-ré*

**swing** **(l') altalena**
*(l') al-ta-LÉ-na*

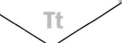

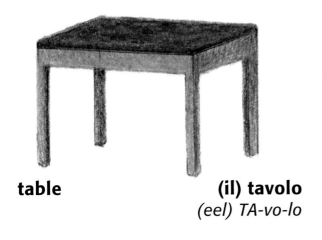

**table**     **(il) tavolo**
*(eel) TA-vo-lo*

**teapot**     **(la) teiera**
*(la) té-EE-È-ra*

**teddy bear**     **(l') orsacchiotto**
*(l') or-sa-KKEE-O-tto*

**television**     **(la) televisione**
*(la) té-lé-vee-SEE-O-né*

**ten**     **dieci**
*DEE-È-tchee*

**tent**     **(la) tenda**
*(la) TÈN-da*

**theater**     **(il ) teatro**
*(eel) té-A-tro*

**thimble**     **(il) ditale**
*(eel) dee-TA-lé*

**(to) think**     **pensare**
*pén-SA-ré*

**three**     **tre**
*tré*

**tie**     **(la) cravatta**
*(la) kra-VA-tta*

**(to) tie**     **allacciare**
*a-lla-TCHA-ré*

**tiger** **(la) tigre**
*(la) TEE-gré*

**toaster** **(il) tostapane**
*(eel) to-sta-PA-né*

**tomato** **(il) pomodoro**
*(eel) po-mo-DO-ro*

**toucan** **(il) tucano**
*(eel) too-KA-no*

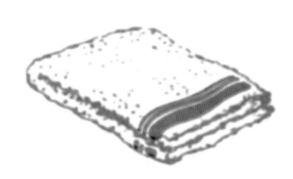

**towel** **(l') asciugamano**
*(l') a-shoo-ga-MA-no*

**tower** **(la) torre**
*(la) TO-rré*

**toy box** **(la) scatola dei giocattoli**
*(la) SKA-to-la dé-ee jo-KA-tto-lee*

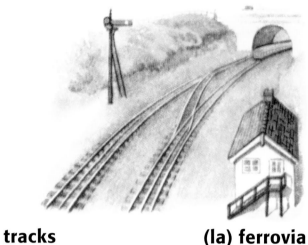

**tracks** **(la) ferrovia**
*(la) fé-rro-VEE-a*

**train station** **(la) stazione**
*(la) sta-ZEE-O-né*

**tray** **(il) vassoio**
*(eel) va-SSO-EE-o*

**tree** **(l') albero**
*(l') AL-be-ro*

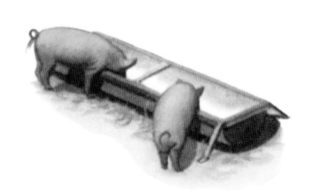

**trough** **(la) mangiatoia**
*(la) man-ja-TO-ee-a*

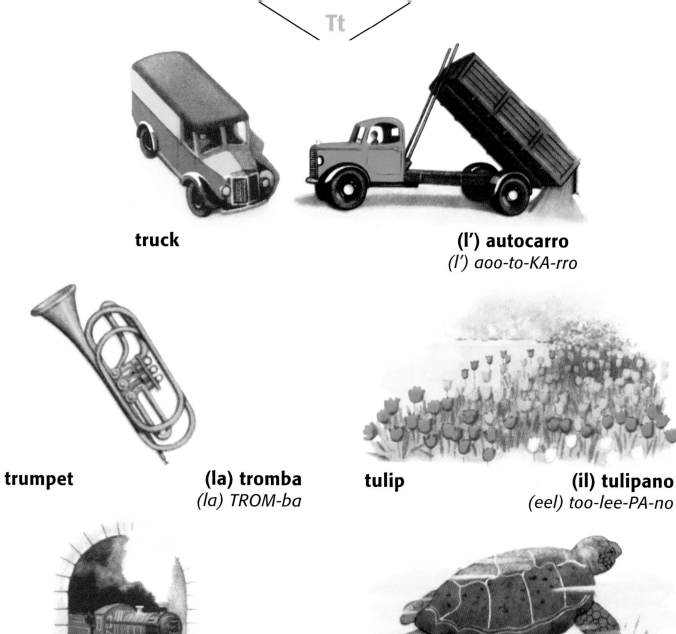

**truck**

**(l') autocarro**
*(l') aoo-to-KA-rro*

**trumpet**       **(la) tromba**
*(la) TROM-ba*

**tulip**       **(il) tulipano**
*(eel) too-lee-PA-no*

**tunnel**       **(il) tunnel**
*(eel) too-NNÈL*

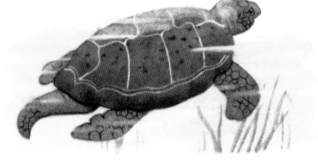

**turtle**       **(la) tartaruga**
*(la) tar-ta-ROO-ga*

**twins**       **(le) gemelle**
*(lé) jé-MÈ-llé*

**two**       **due**
*DOO-é*

**umbrella**   **(l') ombrello**
*(l') om-BRÈ-llo*

**uphill**   **(la) salita**
*(la) sa-LEE-ta*

**vase**   **(il) vaso**
*(eel) VA-so*

**veil**   **(il) velo**
*(eel) VÉ-lo*

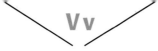

**village**      **(il) villaggio**
*(eel) vee-LLA-jo*

**violet**     **(la) violetta**
*(la) vee-o-LÉ-tta*

**violin**      **(il) violino**
*(eel) vee-o-LEE-no*

**voyage**      **(il) viaggio**
*(eel) vee-A-jo*

**waiter** **(il) cameriere**
*(eel) ka-mé-REE-È-ré*

**(to) wake up** **svegliarsi**
*své-ËAR-see*

**walrus** **(il) tricheco**
*(eel) tree-KÉ-ko*

**(to) wash** **lavare**
*la-VA-ré*

**watch** **(l') orologio**
*(l') o-ro-LO-jo*

**(to) watch** **guardare**
*goo-ar-DA-ré*

**(to) water**      **annaffiare**
*anna-FFEE-a-ré*

**waterfall**      **(la) cascata**
*(la) ka-SKA-ta*

**watering can**      **(l') annaffiatoio**
*(l') a-nna-ffee-a-TO-EE-o*

**watermelon**      **(l') anguria**
*(l') an-GOO-ree-a*

**weather vane**      **(la) banderuola**
*(la) ban-dé-ROO-ola*

**(to) weigh**      **misurare**
*mee-soo-RA-ré*

**whale**       **(la) balena**
*(la) ba-LÉ-na*

**wheel**       **(la) ruota**
*(la) ROO-ota*

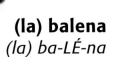

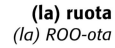

**wheelbarrow**       **(la) cariola**
*(la) ka-ree-O-la*

**whiskers**       **(i) baffi**
*(ee) BA-ffee*

**(to) whisper**       **bisbigliare**
*bee-sbee-ËA-ré*

**whistle**       **(il) fischietto**
*(eel) fee-skee-É-tto*

**white**  **bianco**
*bee-AN-ko*

**wig**  **(la) parrucca**
*(la) pa-RROO-kka*

**wind**  **(il) vento**
*(eel) VÈN-to*

**window**  **(la) finestra**
*(la) fee-NÈ-stra*

**wings**  **(le) ali**
*(lé) A-lee*

**winter**  **(l') inverno**
*(l') een-VÈR-no*

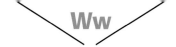

**wolf**

**(il) lupo**
*(eel) LOO-po*

**wood**

**(il) legno**
*(eel) LÉ-ño*

**word**

**(la) parola**
*(la) pa-RO-la*

**(to) write**

**scrivere**
*SKREE-vé-ré*

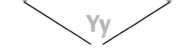

**yellow**

**giallo**
*JA-llo*

**zebra**

**(la) zebra**
*(la) DSÈ-bra*

## A

**abbracciare** (to) hug
**abete** fir tree
**acquario** aquarium
**"Addio"** "Good-bye"
**aeroplano** airplane
**agnellino** lamb
**ago** needle
**albero** tree
**albero di Natale** Christmas tree
**alfabeto** alphabet
**ali** wings
**allacciare** (to) tie
**alligatore** alligator
**altalena** seesaw; swing
**amaca** hammock
**amico** friend
**ananas** pineapple
**anatra** duck
**andar carponi** (to) crawl
**anello** ring
**anguria** watermelon
**annaffiare** (to) water
**annaffiatoio** watering can
**antilope** antelope
**ape** bee
**aperto** open
**aquila** eagle
**aragosta** lobster
**arancia** orange
**arco** arch
**arcobaleno** rainbow
**arrampicarsi** (to) climb
**asciugamano** towel
**ascoltare** (to) listen
**asino** donkey
**atata** potato
**attraversare** (to) cross
**autocarro** truck
**autostrada** highway
**autunno** autumn

## B

**bacheca** bulletin board
**baffi** whiskers
**balena** whale
**ballare** (to) dance
**bambola** doll
**banana** banana
**banco** desk
**banderuola** weather vane
**bandiera** flag
**bar** café
**barca** boat
**bebè** baby
**beccare** (to) peck
**bere** (to) drink
**berretto** cap
**bianco** white
**bicchiere** glass
**bicicletta** bicycle
**binocolo** binoculars
**bisbigliare** (to) whisper
**biscotto** cracker
**blu** blue
**bocca** mouth
**borsetta** handbag
**botte** barrel
**bottiglia** bottle
**braccialetto** bracelet
**brocca** pitcher
**bue** ox
**"Buona notte"** "Good Night"
**bussola** compass
**busta da lettere** envelope

## C

**cacciavite** screwdriver
**cactus** cactus
**calabrone** bumblebee
**calamita** magnet
**cameriere** waiter
**camicia** shirt
**cammello** camel
**campanella** bell

**campo** field
**cancello** gate
**candela** candle
**cane** dog
**canguro** kangaroo
**canoa** canoe
**cantare** (to) sing
**capitano** captain
**cappello** hat
**cappotto** coat
**capra** goat
**cariola** wheelbarrow
**carota** carrot
**carrozza** coach
**carta** card; paper
**cartina geografica** map
**casa della bambola** dollhouse
**casa** house
**cascata** waterfall
**castello** castle
**castoro** beaver
**cavaliere** knight
**cavallo** horse
**cavolo** cabbage
**cerbiatto** deer
**cestino** basket
**cetriolo** cucumber
**cetriolo sottaceto** pickle
**chiave** key
**chitarra** guitar
**cicogna** stork
**ciliegia** cherry
**cinque** five
**cintura** belt
**cioccolata** chocolate
**ciotola** bowl
**ciottolo** pebble
**cipolla** onion
**circo** chimney
**civetta** owl
**clessidra** hourglass
**coccinella** ladybug
**cocco** coconut

**colazione** breakfast
**collana** necklace
**colori** paint
**coltello** knife
**conchiglia** shell
**coniglio** rabbit
**copricapo** headdress
**corda** rope
**corna** horns
**cornice** frame
**corona** crown
**correre** (to) run
**cortina** curtain
**cravatta** tie
**criceto** hamster
**crostata** pie
**cubetti di ghiaccio** ice cubes
**cucchiaio** spoon
**cuccia** doghouse
**cucciolo** puppy
**cucinare** (to) cook
**cucire** (to) sew
**culla** cradle
**cuore** heart
**cuscino** pillow

## D

**dar da mangiare** (to) feed
**dare** (to) give
**data** date
**delfino** dolphin
**dente di leone** dandelion
**deserto** desert
**dieci** ten
**disegnare** (to) draw
**disordinato** messy
**ditale** thimble
**dito** finger
**divano** sofa
**doccia** shower
**dolciume** candy
**dormire** (to) sleep
**drago** dragon
**due** two

## E

**elefante** elephant
**eschimese** eskimo
**esplorare** (to) explore

## F

**fantino** jockey
**farfalla** butterfly
**faro** lighthouse
**fazzoletto** handkerchief
**felce** fern
**ferro da stiro** iron
**ferro di cavallo** horseshoe
**ferrovia** tracks
**fieno** hay
**finestra** window
**fiore** blossom; flower
**fischietto** whistle
**fiume** river
**foglia** leaf
**foglia d'acero** maple leaf
**fontana** fountain
**forbici** scissors
**forchetta** fork
**formaggio** cheese
**fornaio** baker
**fragola** strawberry
**francobollo** stamp
**fratello** brother
**freccia** arrow
**frigorifero** refrigerator
**frutta** fruit
**fumaiolo** chimney
**fungo** mushroom
**fuoco** fire

## G

**gabbia** birdcage
**gabbiano** seagull
**galleggiare** (to) float
**gallina** hen
**gallo** rooster

## (continued)

**gamba** leg
**gattino** kitten
**gatto** cat
**gelato** ice cream
**gemelle** twins
**gente** people
**geranio** geranium
**giacca** jacket
**giallo** yellow
**giardino** garden
**giocare** (to) play
**giocoliere** juggler
**giornaletto** magazine
**giraffa** giraffe
**girasole** sunflower
**globo** globe
**gomito** elbow
**grillo** grasshopper
**grotta** cave
**guanto** glove
**guardare** (to) watch

## I

**idrante** hydrant
**impermeabile** raincoat
**imposta** shutter
**inseparabile** lovebird
**inverno** winter
**iris** iris
**isola** island

## K

**koala** koala bear

## L

**lampada** lamp
**lampadina** lightbulb
**lampone** raspberry
**lattaio** milkman
**lattuga** lettuce

lavanda lavender
lavare (to) wash
lavorare a maglia (to) knit
leccare (to) lap
leggere (to) read
legno wood
leone lion
letto bed
libellula dragonfly
libro book
lillà lilac
limone lemon
lince lynx
locomotiva engine
lucchetto padlock
lumaca snail
luna moon
lupo wolf

## M

macchina car
macchina del gas stove
macchinetta fotografica camera
maglione sweater
maiale pig
malato sick
mamma mother
mangiare (to) eat
mangiatoia trough
mano hand
marinaio sailor
marmellata jam
marrone brown
martello hammer
maschera mask
matita pencil
mattoni blocks
mela apple
melanzana eggplant
mercato marketplace
metropolitana subway
mezzo guanto mitten
miele honey
misurare (to) weigh
mobili furniture
montagna mountain

mostrare (to) show
mucca cow
musica music

## N

nascondersi (to) hide
nave da crociera ocean liner
nave ship
navigare (to) sail
nero black
neve snow
nido nest
nocciolo pit
noce nut
nodo knot
nonna grandmother
nonno grandfather
nove nine
nudo naked
numero number
nuvola cloud

## O

oca goose
occhiali glasses
occhio eye
ombrello umbrella
ornitorinco platypus
orologio watch
orsacchiotto teddy bear
orso bear
orso polare polar bear
orzo barley
osso bone
otto eight

## P

padella pot
pagliaccio clown
pala shovel
palchi antlers
palla ball
palloncino balloon

palma palm tree
panchina bench
pane bread
pannocchia corn
papà father
pappagallo parrot
paracadute parachute
parco park
parola word
parrucca wig
passaporto passport
passero sparrow
passino sieve
pastore shepherd
pattinare sul ghiaccio ice-skating
paura fear
pecora sheep
pedalino sock
pellicano pelican
pensare (to) think
pera pear
pesca peach
pescare (to) fish
pesce fish
pesciolino rosso goldfish
pettine comb
piangere (to) cry
pianoforte piano
piatto plate
piccione pigeon
piccolo small
piede foot

**pinguino** penguin
**pino** pine
**pioggia** rain
**pipistrello** bat
**pittore** painter
**piuma** feather
**piumino** comforter
**pomodoro** tomato
**ponte** bridge
**pony** pony
**porcospino** hedgehog
**portare** (to) carry
**pranzo** lunch
**prestigiatore** magician
**procione** raccoon
**prugna** plum
**pugno** fist
**puzzle** jigsaw puzzle
**pyjama** pajamas

## Q

**quaderno** notebook
**quattro** four
**quotidiano** newspaper

## R

**racchetta** racket
**raccogliere** (to) gather
**raccolto** harvest
**radice** root
**radio** radio
**ragazza** girl
**ragazzo** boy
**ragnatela** spiderweb
**ragno** spider
**rana** frog
**ramo** branch
**ravanello** radish
**razzo** rocket
**regalo** present
**regina** queen
**remare** (to) row
**remo** oar
**righello** ruler
**rinoceronte** rhinoceros

**risata** laughter
**rosa** rose
**rosso** red
**ruota** wheel

## S

**sale** salt
**salita** uphill
**saltare** (to) jump
**sbucciare** (to) peel
**scala** ladder
**scala mobile** escalator
**scale** stairs
**scarabeo** beetle
**scarpa** shoe
**scatola dei giocattoli** toy box
**sciarpa** scarf
**scimmia** monkey
**scoiattolo** squirrel
**scopa** broom
**scrivere** (to) write
**scuola** school
**secchio** bucket
**sedere** (to) sit
**sedia** chair
**sei** six
**sentiero** path
**serpente** snake
**serra** greenhouse

**serratura** lock
**sette** seven
**slitta** sled
**soldi** money
**sole** sun
**sorriso** smile
**spazzare** (to) sweep
**spazzola** brush
**specchio** mirror
**spiaggia** beach
**spilla da balia** safety pin
**spilla** pin
**sporco** dirty
**squalo** shark
**staccionata** fence
**stazione** train station
**stella marina** starfish
**stivale** boot
**strada** road
**strumento** instrument
**struzzo** ostrich
**suonare** (to) ring
**svegliarsi** (to) wake up

## T

**tagliaboschi** lumberjack
**tamburo** drum
**tappeto** carpet
**tappo** cork
**tartaruga** turtle
**tasso** badger
**tavolo** table
**taxi** cab
**teatro** theater
**teiera** teapot
**televisione** television
**tenda** tent
**tetto** roof
**tigre** tiger
**tirare** (to) pull

**Folk Tales from Bohemia**
Adolf Wenig
This folk tale collection is one of a kind, focusing uniquely on humankind's struggle with evil in the world. Delicately ornate red and black text and illustrations set the mood.
*Ages 9 and up*
90 pages • red and black illustrations • 5 1/2 x 8 1/4 • 0-7818-0718-2 • W • $14.95hc • (786)

**Czech, Moravian and Slovak Fairy Tales**
Parker Fillmore
Fifteen different classic, regional folk tales and 23 charming illustrations whisk the reader to places of romance, deception, royalty, and magic.
*Ages 12 and up*
243 pages • 23 b/w illustrations • 5 1/2 x 8 1/4 • 0-7818-0714-X • W • $14.95 hc • (792)

**Glass Mountain: Twenty-Eight Ancient Polish Folk Tales and Fables**
W.S. Kuniczak
Illustrated by Pat Bargielski
As a child in a far-away misty corner of Volhynia, W.S. Kuniczak was carried away to an extraordinary world of magic and illusion by the folk tales of his Polish nurse.
171 pages • 6 x 9 • 8 illustrations • 0-7818-0552-X • W • $16.95hc • (645)

**Old Polish Legends**
Retold by F.C. Anstruther
Wood engravings by J. Sekalski
This fine collection of eleven fairy tales, with an introduction by Zymunt Nowakowski, was first published in Scotland during World War II.
66 pages • 7 1/4 x 9 • 11 woodcut engravings • 0-7818-0521-X • W • $11.95hc • (653)

**Folk Tales from Russia**
by Donald A. Mackenzie
With nearly 200 pages and 8 full-page black-and-white illustrations, the reader will be charmed by these legendary folk tales that symbolically weave magical fantasy with the historic events of Russia's past.
*Ages 12 and up*
192 pages • 8 b/w illustrations • 5 1/2 x 8 1/4 • 0-7818-0696-8 • W • $12.50hc • (788)

**Fairy Gold: A Book of Classic English Fairy Tales**
Chosen by Ernest Rhys
Illustrated by Herbert Cole
Forty-nine imaginative black and white illustrations accompany thirty classic tales, including such beloved stories as "Jack and the Bean Stalk" and "The Three Bears."
*Ages 12 and up*
236 pages • 5 1/2 x 8 1/4 • 49 b/w illustrations • 0-7818-0700-X • W • $14.95hc • (790)

### Tales of Languedoc: From the South of France
Samuel Jacques Brun
For readers of all ages, here is a masterful collection of folk tales from the south of France.
*Ages 12 and up*
248 pages • 33 b/w sketches • 5 1/2 x 8 1/4 • 0-7818-0715-8 • W • $14.95hc • (793)

### Twenty Scottish Tales and Legends
Edited by Cyril Swinson
Illustrated by Allan Stewart
Twenty enchanting stories take the reader to an extraordinary world of magic harps, angry giants, mysterious spells and gallant Knights.
*Ages 9 and up*
215 pages • 5 1/2 x 8 1/4 • 8 b/w illustrations • 0-7818-0701-8 • W • $14.95 hc • (789)

### Swedish Fairy Tales
Translated by H. L. Braekstad
A unique blending of enchantment, adventure, comedy, and romance make this collection of Swedish fairy tales a must-have for any library.
*Ages 9 and up*
190 pages • 21 b/w illustrations • 51/2 x 81/4 • 0-7818-0717-4 • W • $12.50hc • (787)

### The Little Mermaid and Other Tales
Hans Christian Andersen
Here is a near replica of the first American edition of 27 classic fairy tales from the masterful Hans Christian Andersen.
*Ages 9 and up*
508 pages • b/w illustrations • 6 x 9 • 0-7818-0720-4 • W • $19.95hc • (791)

### Pakistani Folk Tales: Toontoony Pie and Other Stories
Ashraf Siddiqui and Marilyn Lerch
Illustrated by Jan Fairservis
In these 22 folk tales are found not only the familiar figures of folklore—kings and beautiful princesses—but the magic of the Far East, cunning jackals, and wise holy men.
*Ages 7 and up*
158 pages • 6 1/2 x 8 1/2 • 38 illustrations • 0-7818-0703-4 • W • $12.50hc • (784)

### Folk Tales from Chile
Brenda Hughes
This selection of 15 tales gives a taste of the variety of Chile's rich folklore. Fifteen charming illustrations accompany the text.
*Ages 7 and up*
121 pages • 5 1/2 x 8 1/4 • 15 illustrations • 0-7818-0712-3 • W • $12.50hc • (785)

All prices subject to change. **To purchase Hippocrene Books** contact your local bookstore, call (718) 454-2366, or write to: HIPPOCRENE BOOKS, 171 Madison Avenue, New York, NY 10016. Please enclose check or money order, adding $5.00 shipping (UPS) for the first book and $.50 for each additional book.